The Traeger Grill Bible

Juicy Recipes To Turn Every Beginner Into The Complete
Pitmaster With Techniques, Strategies, And Tips You Need
To Master Your Wood Pellet Grill

Grill Academy

or implied. Readers acknowledge that the author is not engaging in the rendering of legal, financial, medical or professional advice. The content within this book has been derived from various sources. Please consult a licensed professional before attempting any techniques outlined in this book.

By reading this document, the reader agrees that under no circumstances is the author responsible for any losses, direct or indirect, which are incurred as a result of the use of information contained within this document, including, but not limited to, — errors, omissions, or inaccuracies.

Table of Contents

CHAPTER 1: Beef Recipes... 9

   1. Traeger Smoked Rib-eye Steaks 10

   2. Traeger Grill Deli-Style Roast Beef................................. 12

   3. Traeger Beef Jerky 14

   4. Traeger Smoked Beef Roast... 16

   5. Traeger Beef Tenderloin 18

   6. Trager New York Strip.. 20

   7. Traeger Stuffed Peppers 22

   8. Traeger Prime Rib Roast 24

CHAPTER 2: Pork Recipes... 27

   9. Barbecued Tenderloin 27

   10. Lovable Pork Belly... 29

CHAPTER 3: Lamb Recipes 32

   11. Traeger Smoked Lamb Shoulder................................. 32

   12. Traeger Smoked Pulled Lamb Sliders.......................... 34

   13. Traeger Smoked Lamb Meatballs 36

   14. Traeger Crown Rack of Lamb...................................... 38

CHAPTER 4: Seafood Recipes... 41

   15. Traeger Grilled Lingcod... 42

   16. Crab Stuffed Lingcod... 44

   17. Traeger Smoked Shrimp 47

   18. Grilled Shrimp Kabobs 49

CHAPTER 5: Vegetarian Recipes 52

   19. Smoked and Smashed New Potatoes........................... 53

   20. Smoked Brussels Sprouts.. 55

   21. Apple Veggie Burger 57

22. Smoked Tofu 59

23. Easy Smoked Vegetables 60

24. Zucchini with Red Potatoes 62

25. Shiitake Smoked Mushrooms 64

26. Garlic and Herb Smoke Potato 66

CHAPTER 6: Vegan Recipes 69

27. Wood Pellet Grilled Zucchini Squash Spears 70

28. Wood Pellet Cold Smoked Cheese....................................... 72

29. Wood Pellet Grilled Asparagus and Honey Glazed Carrots 74

CHAPTER 7: Poultry Recipes 77

30. Lemon Cornish Chicken Stuffed with Crab 77

31. Bacon Cordon Blue 79

32. Roast Duck à I Orange.. 81

33. Herb Roasted Turkey 83

CHAPTER 8: Appetizer.. 86

34. Bacon Cheddar Slider.. 86

35. Garlic Parmesan Wedge... 89

36. Roasted Vegetables 91

37. Grilled Mushroom Skewers 93

CHAPTER 9: Dessert Recipe 97

38. S'mores Dip... 98

39. Bacon Chocolate Chip Cookies 100

40. Cinnamon Sugar Pumpkin Seeds 102

41. Apple Cobbler 103

42. Pineapple Cake 105

CHAPTER 10: Extra Recipes.. 108

43. Ultimate Lamb Burgers 108

44. Citrus- Smoked Trout.. 110

45. Sunday Supper Salmon with Olive Tapenade 112

46. Grilled Tuna... 115

47. Grilled Swordfish.. 117

48. Lamb Kebabs.. 119

49. Special Occasion's Dinner Cornish Hen 121

50. Crispy and Juicy Chicken 123

CHAPTER 1:
Beef Recipes

1. Traeger Smoked Rib-eye Steaks

Preparation Time: 15 minutes

Cooking Time: 35 minutes

Servings: 1

Ingredients:

- 2-inch-thick rib-eye steaks
- Steak rub of choice

Direction:

1. Preheat your Traeger grill to low smoke.
2. Sprinkle the steak with your favorite steak rub and place it on the grill. Let it smoke for 25 minutes.
3. Remove the steak from the grill and set the temperature to 400°F.
4. Return the steak to the grill and sear it for 5 minutes on each side.
5. Cook until the desired temperature is achieved; 125°F-rare, 145°F-Medium, and 165°F.-Well done.
6. Wrap the steak with foil and let rest for 10 minutes before serving. Enjoy.

Nutrition:

- Calories 225
- Total fat 10.4g

- Protein 32.5g
- Sugar 0g
- Fiber 0g
- Sodium: 63mg

2. Traeger Grill Deli-Style Roast Beef

Preparation Time: 15 minutes

Cooking Time: 4 hours

Servings: 2

Ingredients:

- 4lb round-bottomed roast
- 1 Tablespoon coconut oil
- 1/4 Tablespoon garlic powder; 1/4 Tablespoon onion powder
- 1/4 Tablespoon thyme; 1/4 Tablespoon oregano
- 1/2 Tablespoon paprika; 1/2 Tablespoon salt
- 1/2 Tablespoon black pepper

Direction:

1. Combine all the dry hubs to get a dry rub.
2. Roll the roast in oil then coat with the rub.
3. Set your grill to 185°F and place the roast on the grill.
4. Smoke for 4 hours or until the internal temperature reaches 140°F.
5. Remove the roast from the grill and let rest for 10 minutes.
6. Slice thinly and serve.

Nutrition:

- Calories 90
- Total fat 3g
- Protein 14g
- Sugar 0g
- Fiber 0g
- Sodium: 420mg

3. Traeger Beef Jerky

Preparation Time: 15 minutes

Cooking Time: 5 hours

Servings: 10

Ingredients:

- 3 lb. sirloin steaks;
- 2 cups soy sauce
- 1 cup pineapple juice;
- 1/2 cup brown sugar
- 2 tbsp sriracha; 2 tbsp hoisin
- 2 tbsp red pepper flake
- 2 tbsp rice wine vinegar
- 2 tbsp onion powder

Directions:

1. Mix the marinade in a zip lock bag and add the beef. Mix until well coated and remove as much air as possible.
2. Place the bag in a fridge and let marinate overnight or for 6 hours. Remove the bag from the fridge an hour prior to cooking
3. Startup the Traeger and set it on the smoking settings or at 1900F.

4. Lay the meat on the grill leaving a half-inch space between the pieces. Let cool for 5 hours and turn after 2 hours.

5. Remove from the grill and let cool. Serve or refrigerate

Nutrition:

Calories 309   Total fat 7g   Saturated fat 3g

Total carbs 20g   Net carbs 19g   Protein 34g

Sugars 15g   Fiber 1g   Sodium 2832mg

4. Traeger Smoked Beef Roast

Preparation Time: 10 minutes

Cooking Time: 6 hours

Servings: 6

Ingredients:

- 1-3/4 lb. beef sirloin tip roast
- 1/2 cup BBQ rub
- 2 bottles amber beer
- 1 bottle BBQ sauce

Directions:

1. Turn the Traeger onto the smoke setting.
2. Rub the beef with BBQ rub until well coated then place on the grill. Let smoke for 4 hours while flipping every 1 hour.
3. Transfer the beef to a pan and add the beer. The beef should be 1/2 way covered.
4. Braise the beef until fork tender. It will take 3 hours on the stovetop and 60 minutes on the instant pot.
5. Remove the beef from the ban and reserve 1 cup of the cooking liquid.
6. Use 2 forks to shred the beef into small pieces then return to the pan with the reserved braising liquid.

7. Add BBQ sauce and stir well then keep warm until serving. You can also reheat if it gets cold.

Nutrition:

Calories 829   Total fat 46g   Saturated fat 18g

Total carbs 4g   Net carbs 4g   Protein 86g

Sugars 0g   Fiber 0g   Sodium 181mmg

5. Traeger Beef Tenderloin

Preparation Time: 10 minutes

Cooking Time: 45 minutes

Servings: 6

Ingredients:

- 4 lb. beef tenderloin
- 3 tbsp steak rub
- 1 tbsp kosher salt

Directions:

1. Preheat the Traeger to high heat.
2. Meanwhile, trim excess fat from the beef and cut it into 3 pieces.
3. Coat the steak with rub and kosher salt. Place it on the grill.
4. Close the lid and cook for 10 minutes. Open the lid, flip the beef and cook for 10 more minutes.
5. Reduce the temperature of the grill until 225oF and smoke the beef until the internal temperature reaches 130oF.
6. Remove the beef from the grill and let rest for 15 minutes before slicing and serving.

Nutrition:

Calories 999   Total fat 76g   Saturated fat 30g
Total carbs 0g   Net carbs 0g   Protein 74g
Sugars 0g   Fiber 0g   Sodium 1234mmg

6. Trager New York Strip
Preparation Time: 5 minutes

Cooking Time: 15 minutes

Servings: 6

Ingredients:

- 3 New York strips
- Salt and pepper

Directions:

1. If the steak is in the fridge, remove it 30 minutes prior to cooking.

2. Preheat the Traeger to 450oF.

3. Meanwhile, season the steak generously with salt and pepper. Place it on the grill and let it cook for 5 minutes per side or until the internal temperature reaches 128oF.

4. Remove the steak from the grill and let it rest for 10 minutes.

Nutrition:

- Calories 198
- Total fat 14g
- Saturated fat 6g
- Total carbs 0g
- Net carbs 0g
- Protein 17g
- Sugars 0g
- Fiber 0g
- Sodium 115mg

7. Traeger Stuffed Peppers

Preparation Time: 20 minutes

Cooking Time: 5 hours

Servings: 6

Ingredients:

- 3 bell peppers, sliced in halves ; 1 lb. ground beef, lean
- 1 onion, chopped; 1/2 tbsp red pepper flakes
- 1/2 tbsp salt; 1/4 tbsp pepper
- 1/2 tbsp garlic powder; 1/2 tbsp onion powder
- 1/2 cup white rice; 15 oz stewed tomatoes
- 8 oz tomato sauce; cups cabbage, shredded
- 1-1/2 cup water; 2 cups cheddar cheese

Directions:

1. Arrange the pepper halves on a baking tray and set aside.
2. Preheat your grill to 3250F.
3. Brown the meat in a large skillet. Add onions, pepper flakes, salt, pepper garlic, and onion and cook until the meat is well cooked.
4. Add rice, stewed tomatoes, tomato sauce, cabbage, and water. Cover and simmer until the rice is well cooked, the cabbage is tender and there is no water in the rice.

5. Place the cooked beef mixture in the pepper halves and top with cheese. Place in the grill and cook for 30 minutes.

6. Serve immediately and enjoy it.

Nutrition:

Calories 422   Total fat 22g   Saturated fat 11g   Total carbs 24g

Net carbs 19g   Protein 34g   Sugars 11g   Fiber 5g Sodium 855mg

8. Traeger Prime Rib Roast

Preparation Time: 10 minutes

Cooking Time: 2 hours

Servings: 8

Ingredients:

- lb. rib roast, boneless; 4 tbsp salt; 1 tbsp black pepper
- 1-1/2 tbsp onion powder; 1 tbsp granulated garlic; 1 tbsp rosemary
- 1 cup chopped onion; 1/2 cup carrots, chopped
- 1/2 cup celery, chopped; 2 cups beef broth

Directions:

1. Remove the beef from the fridge 1 hour prior to cooking.
2. Preheat the Traeger to 250oF.
3. In a small mixing bowl, mix salt, pepper, onion, garlic, and rosemary to create your rub.
4. Generously coat the roast with the rub and set it aside.
5. Combine chopped onions, carrots, and celery in a cake pan then place the bee on top.
6. Place the cake pan in the middle of the Traeger and cook for 1 hour.

7. Pour the beef broth at the bottom of the cake pan and cook until the internal temperature reaches 1200F.

8. Remove the cake pan from the Traeger and let rest for 20 minutes before slicing the meat.

9. Pour the cooking juice through a strainer, then skim off any fat at the top. Serve the roast with the cooking juices.

Nutrition:

Calories 721 Total fat 60g Saturated fat 18g Total carbs 3g

Net carbs 2g   Protein 43g   Sugars 1g   Fiber 1g Sodium 2450mmg

CHAPTER 2:
Pork Recipes

9. Barbecued Tenderloin

Preparation Time: 5 minutes

Cooking Time: 30 minutes

Servings: 4-6

Ingredients:

- 2 (1-pound) pork tenderloins
- 1 batch Sweet and Spicy Cinnamon Rub

Directions:

1. Supply your smoker with wood pellets and follow the manufacturer's specific start-up procedure. Preheat the grill

2. Generously season the tenderloins with the rub. Work rubs onto meat.

3. Place the tenderloins and smoke internal temperature reaches 145°F.

4. As you put out the tenderloins from the grill, let it cool down for 5-10 minutes before slicing it up and serving it

Nutrition:

- Calories: 186 Cal
- Fat: 4 g
- Carbohydrates: 8 g
- Protein: 29 g
- Fiber: 1 g

10. Lovable Pork Belly

Preparation Time: 15 Minutes

Cooking Time: 4 Hours and 30 Minutes

Servings: 4

Ingredients:

- 5 pounds of pork belly; 1 cup dry rub
- 3 tablespoons olive oil

For Sauce

- Two tablespoons honey
- Three tablespoons butter
- 1 cup BBQ sauce

Directions:

1. Take your drip pan and add water. Cover with aluminum foil.
2. Pre-heat your smoker to 250 degrees F
3. Add pork cubes, dry rub, olive oil into a bowl and mix well
4. Use water fill water pan halfway through and place it over drip pan.
5. Add wood chips to the side tray
6. Transfer pork cubes to your smoker and smoke for 3 hours (covered)

7. Remove pork cubes from the smoker and transfer to foil pan, add honey, butter, BBQ sauce, and stir

8. Cover the pan with foil and move back to a smoker, smoke for 90 minutes more

9. Remove foil and smoke for 15 minutes more until the sauce thickens

10. Serve and enjoy!

Nutrition:

Calories: 1164   Fat: 68g   Carbohydrates: 12g Protein: 104g

CHAPTER 3:
Lamb Recipes

11. Traeger Smoked Lamb Shoulder

Preparation Time: 20 Minutes

Cooking Time: 3 Hours

Servings: 7

Ingredients:

- 5 lb. lamb shoulder; 1 cup cider vinegar

- 2 tbsp. oil; 2 tbsp. kosher salt

- 2 tbsp. black pepper, freshly ground

- 1 tbsp. dried rosemary

For the Spritz

- 1 cup apple cider vinegar

- 1 cup apple juice

Directions:

1. Preheat the Traeger to 225oF with a pan of water for moisture.

2. Trim any extra fat from the lamb and rinse the meat in cold water. Pat dry with a paper towel.

3. Inject the cider vinegar in the meat, then pat dry with a clean paper towel.

4. Rub the meat with oil, salt, black pepper, and dried rosemary. Tie the lamb shoulder with a twine.

5. Place in the smoker for an hour, then spritz after every 15 minutes until the internal temperature reaches 1650F.

6. Remove from the Traeger and let rest for 1 hour before shredding and serving.

Nutrition:

Calories 472   Total Fat 37g   Total carbs 3g   Protein 31g   Sodium 458mg

12. Traeger Smoked Pulled Lamb Sliders

Preparation Time: 10 Minutes

Cooking Time: 9 Hours

Servings: 7

Ingredients:

- 5 lb. lamb shoulder, boneless
- 1/2 cup olive oil; 1/3 cup kosher salt
- 1/3 cup pepper, coarsely ground
- 1/3 cup granulated garlic

For the spritz

- 4 oz Worcestershire sauce
- 6 oz apple cider vinegar

Directions:

1. Preheat the Traeger to 2250F with a pan of water for moisture.

2. Trim any excess fat from the lamb, then pat it dry with some paper towel. Rub with oil, salt, pepper, and garlic.

3. Place the lamb in the Traeger smoker for 90 minutes, then spritz every 30 minutes until the internal temperature reaches 1650F.

4. Transfer the lamb to a foil pan, then add the remaining spritz liquid. Cover with a foil and place back in the Traeger.

5. Smoke until the internal temperature reaches 2050F.

6. Remove from the smoker and let rest in a cooler without ice for 30 minutes before pulling it. Serve with slaw or bun and enjoy.

Nutrition:

Calories 235 Total Fat 6g Total Carbs 22g Protein 20g

Sugars 7g   Fiber 1g   Sodium 592mg   Potassium 318mg

13. Traeger Smoked Lamb Meatballs

Preparation Time: 10 Minutes

Cooking Time: 1 Hour

Servings: 20 Meatballs

Ingredients:

- 1 lb. lamb shoulder, ground
- Three garlic cloves, finely diced
- 3 tbsp. shallot, diced
- 1 tbsp. salt; One egg
- 1/2 tbsp. pepper; 1/2 tbsp. cumin
- 1/2 tbsp. smoked paprika
- 1/4 tbsp. red pepper flakes
- 1/4 tbsp. cinnamon
- 1/4 cup panko breadcrumbs

Directions:

1. Set your Traeger to 250oF.
2. Combine all the fixings in a small bowl, then mix thoroughly using your hands.
3. Form golf ball-sized meatballs and place them on a baking sheet.
4. Place the baking sheet in the smoker and smoke until the internal temperature reaches 160oF.

5. Remove the meatballs from the smoker and serve when hot.

Nutrition:

Calories 93   Total fat 5.9g   Total carbs 4.8g

Protein 5g   Sugars 0.3g   Fiber 0.3g

Sodium 174.1mg   Potassium 82.8mg

14. Traeger Crown Rack of Lamb
Preparation Time: 30 Minutes

Cooking Time: 30 Minutes

Servings: 6

Ingredients:

- Two racks of lamb. Frenched
- 1 tbsp garlic, crushed; 1 tbsp rosemary
- 1/2 cup olive oil; Kitchen twine

Directions:

1. Preheat your Traeger to 4500F.
2. Rinse the lab with clean cold water, then pat it dry with a paper towel.
3. Lay the lamb even on a chopping board and score a ¼ inch down between the bones. Repeat the process between the bones on each lamb rack. Set aside.
4. In a small mixing bowl, combine garlic, rosemary, and oil. Brush the lamb rack generously with the mixture.
5. Bend the lamb rack into a semicircle, then place the racks together such that the bones will be up and will form a crown shape.
6. Wrap around four times, starting from the base moving upward. Tie tightly to keep the racks together.

7. Place the lambs on a baking sheet and set in the Traeger. Cook on high heat for 10 minutes. Reduce the temperature to 300oF and cook for 20 more minutes or until the internal temperature reaches 130oF.

8. Remove the lamb rack from the Traeger and let rest while wrapped in a foil for 15 minutes. Serve when hot.

Nutrition:

Calories 390 Total fat 35g Total carbs 0g Protein 17g Sodium 65mg

CHAPTER 4:
Seafood Recipes

15. Traeger Grilled Lingcod

Preparation Time: 10 Minutes

Cooking Time: 15 Minutes

Servings: 6

Ingredients:

- 2 lb. lingcod fillets
- 1/2 tbsp salt
- 1/2 tbsp white pepper
- 1/4 tbsp cayenne pepper
- Lemon wedges

Directions:

1. Preheat your Traeger to 3750F.
2. Place the lingcod on a parchment paper or a grill mat
3. Season the fish with salt, pepper, and top with lemon wedges.
4. Cook the fish for 15 minutes or until the internal temperature reaches 1450F.

Nutrition:

- Calories 245
- Total fat 2g

- Total carbs 2g
- Protein 52g
- Sugars 1g
- Fiber 1g
- Sodium 442mg

16. Crab Stuffed Lingcod

Preparation Time: 20 Minutes

Cooking Time: 30 Minutes

Servings: 6

Ingredients:

Lemon cream sauce

- Four garlic cloves; One shallot; One leek
- 2 tbsp olive oil; 1 tbsp salt; 1/4 tbsp black pepper
- 3 tbsp butter; 1/4 cup white wine; 1 cup whipping cream
- 2 tbsp lemon juice; 1 tbsp lemon zest

Crab mix

- 1 lb. crab meat; 1/3 cup mayo
- 1/3 cup sour cream; 1/3 cup lemon cream sauce
- 1/4 green onion, chopped; 1/4 tbsp black pepper
- 1/2 tbsp old bay seasoning

Fish

- 2 lb. lingcod; 1 tbsp olive oil
- 1 tbsp salt; 1 tbsp paprika
- 1 tbsp green onion, chopped

- 1 tbsp Italian parsley

Directions:

Lemon cream sauce

1. Chop garlic, shallot, and leeks, then add to a saucepan with oil, salt, pepper, and butter.

2. Sauté over medium heat until the shallot is translucent.

3. Deglaze with white wine, then add whipping cream. Bring the sauce to boil, reduce heat, and simmer for 3 minutes.

4. Remove from heat and add lemon juice and lemon zest. Transfer the sauce to a blender and blend until smooth.

5. Set aside 1/3 cup for the crab mix

Crab mix

1. Add all the fixings to a mixing bowl and mix thoroughly until well combined.

2. Set aside

Fish

1. Fire up your Traeger to high heat, then slice the fish into 6-ounce portions.

2. Lay the fish on its side on a cutting board and slice it 3/4 way through the middle leaving a 1/2 inch on each end to have a nice pouch.

3. Rub the oil into the fish, then place them on a baking sheet. Sprinkle with salt.

4. Stuff crab mix into each fish, then sprinkle paprika and place it on the grill.

5. Cook for 15 minutes or more if the fillets are more than 2 inches thick.

6. Remove the fish and transfer to serving platters. Pour the remaining lemon cream sauce on each fish and garnish with onions and parsley.

Nutrition:

Calories 476   Total fat 33g

Saturated fat 14g   Total carbs 6g

Net carbs 5g   Protein 38g

Sugars 3g   Fiber 1g

Sodium 1032mg

17. Traeger Smoked Shrimp

Preparation Time: 10 Minutes

Cooking Time: 10 Minutes

Servings: 6

Ingredients:

- 1 lb. tail-on shrimp, uncooked
- 1/2 tbsp onion powder
- 1/2 tbsp garlic powder
- 1/2 tbsp salt
- 4 tbsp teriyaki sauce
- 2 tbsp green onion, minced
- 4 tbsp sriracha mayo

Directions:

1. Peel the shrimp shells leaving the tail on, then wash well and rise.
2. Drain well and pat dry with a paper towel.
3. Preheat your Traeger to 4500F.
4. Season the shrimp with onion powder, garlic powder, and salt. Place the shrimp in the Traeger and cook for 6 minutes on each side.
5. Remove the shrimp from the Traeger and toss with teriyaki sauce, then garnish with onions and mayo.

Nutrition:

- Calories 87
- Total carbs 2g
- Net carbs 2g
- Protein 16g
- Sodium 1241mg

18. Grilled Shrimp Kabobs

Preparation Time: 5 Minutes

Cooking Time: 10 Minutes

Servings: 4

Ingredients:

- 1 lb. colossal shrimp, peeled and deveined
- 2 tbsp. oil
- 1/2 tbsp. garlic salt
- 1/2 tbsp. salt
- 1/8 tbsp. pepper
- Six skewers

Directions:

1. Preheat your Traeger to 3750F.
2. Pat the shrimp dry with a paper towel.
3. In a mixing bowl, mix oil, garlic salt, salt, and pepper
4. Toss the shrimp in the mixture until well coated.
5. Skewer the shrimps and cook in the Traeger with the lid closed for 4 minutes.
6. Open the lid, flip the skewers, cook for another 4 minutes, or wait until the shrimp is pink and the flesh is opaque.
7. Serve.

Nutrition:

- Calories 325
- Protein 20g
- Sodium 120mg

CHAPTER 5:
Vegetarian Recipes

19. Smoked and Smashed New Potatoes

Preparation Time: 5 minutes

Cooking Time: 8 hours

Servings: 4

Ingredients:

- 1-1/2 pounds small new red potatoes or fingerlings
- Extra virgin olive oil
- Sea salt and black pepper
- 2 tbsp softened butter

Directions:

1. Let the potatoes dry. Once dried, put in a pan and coat with salt, pepper, and extra virgin olive oil.
2. Place the potatoes on the topmost rack of the smoker.
3. Smoke for 60 minutes.
4. Once done, take them out and smash each one
5. Mix with butter and season

Nutrition:

- Calories: 258 Cal
- Fat: 2.0 g

- Carbohydrates: 15.5 g
- Protein: 4.1 g
- Fiber: 1.5 g

20. Smoked Brussels Sprouts

Preparation Time: 15 minutes

Cooking Time: 45 minutes

Servings: 6

Ingredients:

- 1-1/2 pounds Brussels sprouts
- 2 cloves of garlic minced
- 2 tbsp extra virgin olive oil
- Sea salt and cracked black pepper

Directions:

1. Rinse sprouts
2. Remove the outer leaves and brown bottoms off the sprouts.
3. Place sprouts in a large bowl then coat with olive oil.
4. Add a coat of garlic, salt, and pepper and transfer them to the pan.
5. Add to the top rack of the smoker with water and woodchips.
6. Smoke for 45 minutes or until reaches 250 F temperature.
7. Serve

Nutrition:

- Calories: 84 Cal
- Fat: 4.9 g
- Carbohydrates: 7.2 g
- Protein: 2.6 g
- Fiber: 2.9 g

21. Apple Veggie Burger

Preparation Time: 10 minutes

Cooking Time: 35 minutes

Servings: 6

Ingredients:

- 3 tbsp ground flax or ground chia; 1/3 cup of warm water
- 1/2 cups rolled oats; 1 cup chickpeas, drained and rinsed
- 1 tsp cumin; 1/2 cup onion
- 1 tsp dried basil; 2 granny smith apples
- 1/3 cup parsley or cilantro, chopped
- 2 tbsp soy sauce; 2 tsp liquid smoke
- 2 cloves garlic, minced; 1 tsp chili powder
- 1/4 tsp black pepper

Directions:

1. Preheat the smoker to 225°F while adding wood chips and water to it.
2. In a separate bowl, add chickpeas and mash. Mix together the remaining ingredients along with the dipped flax seeds.
3. Form patties from this mixture.
4. Put the patties on the rack of the smoker and smoke them for 20 minutes on each side.

5. When brown, take them out, and serve.

Nutrition:

Calories: 241 Cal   Fat: 5 g   Fiber: 10.3 g

Carbohydrates: 40 g   Protein: 9 g

22. Smoked Tofu

Preparation Time: 10 minutes

Cooking Time: 41 hour and 30 minutes

Servings: 4

Ingredients:

- 400g plain tofu
- Sesame oil

Directions:

1. Preheat the smoker to 225°F while adding wood chips and water to it.
2. Till that time, take the tofu out of the packet and let it rest
3. Slice the tofu in one-inch-thick pieces and apply sesame oil
4. Place the tofu inside the smoker for 45 minutes while adding water and wood chips after one hour.
5. Once cooked, take them out and serve!

Nutrition:

- Calories: 201 Cal
- Fat: 13 g
- Carbohydrates: 1 g
- Protein: 20 g
- Fiber: 0 g

23. Easy Smoked Vegetables

Preparation Time: 15 minutes

Cooking Time: 1 ½ hour

Servings: 6

Ingredients:

- 1 cup of pecan wood chips; 1 medium yellow squash, 1/2-inch slices
- 1 ear fresh corn, silk strands removed, and husks, cut corn into 1-inch pieces
- 1 small red onion, thin wedges; 1 small green bell pepper, 1-inch strips
- 1 small red bell pepper, 1-inch strips
- 1 small yellow bell pepper, 1-inch strips; 1 cup mushrooms, halved
- 2 tbsp vegetable oil; vgetable seasonings

Directions:

1. Take a large bowl and toss all the vegetables together in it.
2. Sprinkle it with seasoning and coat all the vegetables well with it.
3. Place the wood chips and a bowl of water in the smoker.
4. Preheat the smoker at 100°F or ten minutes.

5. Put the vegetables in a pan and add to the middle rack of the electric smoker.

6. Smoke for thirty minutes until the vegetable becomes tender.

7. When done, serve, and enjoy.

Nutrition:

Calories: 97 Cal   Fat: 5 g   Fiber: 3 g

Carbohydrates: 11 g   Protein: 2 g

24. Zucchini with Red Potatoes
Preparation Time: 15 minutes

Cooking Time: 4 hours

Servings: 4

Ingredients:

- 2 zucchinis, sliced in 3/4-inch-thick disks
- 1 red pepper, cut into strips
- 2 yellow squash, sliced in 3/4-inch-thick disks
- 1 medium red onion, cut into wedges
- 6 small red potatoes, cut into chunks; Balsamic Vinaigrette:
- 1/3 cup extra virgin olive oil; 1/4 teaspoon salt
- 1/4 cup balsamic vinegar; 2 tsp Dijon mustard
- 1/8 teaspoon pepper

Directions:

1. For Vinaigrette: Take a medium-sized bowl and blend together olive oil, Dijon mustard, salt, pepper, and balsamic vinegar.
2. Place all the veggies into a large bowl and pour the vinaigrette mixture over it and evenly toss.
3. Put the vegetable in a pan and then smoke for 4 hours at a temperature of 225°F.
4. Serve and enjoy the food.

Nutrition:

Calories: 381 Cal   Fat: 17.6 g   Fiber: 6.5 g
Carbohydrates: 49 g   Protein: 6.7 g

25. Shiitake Smoked Mushrooms

Preparation Time: 15 minutes

Cooking Time: 45 minutes

Servings: 4-6

Ingredients:

- 4 Cup Shiitake Mushrooms
- 1 tbsp canola oil
- 1 tsp onion powder
- 1 tsp granulated garlic
- 1 tsp salt
- 1 tsp pepper

Directions:

1. Combine all the ingredients together
2. Apply the mix over the mushrooms generously.
3. Preheat the smoker at 180°F. Add wood chips and half a bowl of water in the side tray.
4. Place it in the smoker and smoke for 45 minutes.
5. Serve warm and enjoy.

Nutrition:

- Calories: 301 Cal
- Fat: 9 g
- Carbohydrates: 47.8 g
- Protein: 7.1 g
- Fiber: 4.8 g

26. Garlic and Herb Smoke Potato

Preparation Time: 5 minutes

Cooking Time: 2 hours

Servings: 6

Ingredients:

- 1.5 pounds bag of Gemstone Potatoes
- 1/4 cup Parmesan, fresh grated; For the Marinade
- 2 tbsp olive oil; 6 garlic cloves, freshly chopped
- 1/2 tsp dried oregano; 1/2 tsp dried basil
- 1/2 tsp dried dill; 1/2 tsp salt
- 1/2 tsp dried Italian seasoning; 1/4 tsp ground pepper

Directions:

1. Preheat the smoker to 225°F.
2. Wash the potatoes thoroughly and add them to a sealable plastic bag.
3. Add garlic cloves, basil, salt, Italian seasoning, dill, oregano, and olive oil to the zip lock bag. Shake.
4. Place in the fridge for 2 hours to marinate.

5. Next, take an Aluminum foil and put 2 tbsp of water along with the coated potatoes. Fold the foil so that the potatoes are sealed in

6. Place in the preheated smoker. Smoke for 2 hours

7. Remove the foil and pour the potatoes into a bowl.

8. Serve with grated Parmesan cheese.

Nutrition:

Calories: 146 Cal   Fat: 6 g   Fiber: 2.1 g

Carbohydrates: 19 g   Protein: 4 g

CHAPTER 6:
Vegan Recipes

27. Wood Pellet Grilled Zucchini Squash Spears

Preparation Time: 5 minutes,

Cooking Time: 10 minutes.

Servings: 5

Ingredients:

- 4 zucchinis, cleaned and ends cut
- 2 tbsp. olive oil
- 1 tbsp. sherry vinegar
- 2 thyme leaves pulled
- Salt and pepper to taste

Directions:

1. Cut the zucchini into halves then cut each half thirds.
2. Add the rest of the ingredients in a zip lock bag with the zucchini pieces. Toss to mix well.
3. Preheat the wood pellet temperature to 350°F with the lid closed for 15 minutes.
4. Remove the zucchini from the bag and place them on the grill grate with the cut side down.
5. Cook for 4 minutes until the zucchini are tender
6. Remove from grill and serve with thyme leaves. Enjoy.

Nutrition:

Calories: 74 | Fat: 5.4g

Carbs: 6.1g | Protein: 2.6g

Sugar: 3.9g | Fiber: 2.3g

Sodium: 302mg | Potassium: 599mg:

28. Wood Pellet Cold Smoked Cheese

Preparation Time: 5 minutes

Cooking Time: 2 minutes

Servings: 10

Ingredients:

- Ice
- 1 aluminum pan, full-size and disposable
- 1 aluminum pan, half-size, and disposable
- Toothpicks
- A block of cheese

Directions:

1. Preheat the wood pellet to 165°F with the lid closed for 15 minutes.
2. Place the small pan in the large pan. Fill the surrounding of the small pan with ice.
3. Place the cheese in the small pan on top of toothpicks then place the pan on the grill and close the lid.
4. Smoke cheese for 1 hour, flip the cheese, and smoke for 1 more hour with the lid closed.
5. Remove the cheese from the grill and wrap it in parchment paper. Store in the fridge for 2 3 days for the smoke flavor to mellow.
6. Remove from the fridge and serve. Enjoy.

Nutrition:

Calories: 1910 | Total Fat: 7g | Saturated Fat: 6g

Total Carbs: 2g | Net Carbs: 2g | Protein: 6g

Sugar: 1g | Fiber: 0g | Sodium: 340mg | Potassium: 0mg

29. Wood Pellet Grilled Asparagus and Honey Glazed Carrots

Preparation Time: 15 minutes

Cooking Time: 35 minutes

Servings: 5

Ingredients:

- 1 bunch asparagus, trimmed ends
- 1 lb. carrots, peeled
- 2 tbsp. olive oil
- Sea salt to taste
- 2 tbsp. honey
- Lemon zest

Directions:

1. Sprinkle the asparagus with oil and sea salt. Drizzle the carrots with honey and salt.

2. Preheat the wood pellet to 165°F with the lid closed for 15 minutes.

3. Place the carrots in the wood pellet and cook for 15 minutes. Add asparagus and cook for 20 more minutes or until cooked through.

4. Top the carrots and asparagus with lemon zest. Enjoy.

Nutrition:

Calories: 1680 | Total Fat: 30g

Saturated Fat: 2g | Total Carbs: 10g

Net Carbs: 10g | Protein: 4g | Sodium: 514mg

CHAPTER 7:
Poultry Recipes

30. Lemon Cornish Chicken Stuffed with Crab

Preparation Time: 30 minutes (additional 2-3 hours marinade)

Cooking Time: 1 hour 30 minutes

Servings: 2-4

Ingredients:

- 2 Cornish chickens (about 1¾ pound each)
- Half lemon, half
- 4 tbsp western rub or poultry rub
- 2 cups stuffed with crab meat

Directions:

1. Set wood pellet smoker grill for indirect cooking and preheat to 375 ° F with pellets.
2. Place the stuffed animal on the rack in the baking dish. If you do not have a rack that is small enough to fit, you can also place the chicken directly on the baking dish.
3. Roast the chicken at 375 ° F until the inside temperature of the thickest part of the chicken breast reaches 170 ° F, the thigh reaches 180 ° F, and the juice is clear.

4. Test the crab meat stuffing to see if the temperature has reached 165 ° F.

5. Place the roasted chicken under a loose foil tent for 15 minutes before serving.

Nutrition:

Calories 956 | Total fat 47g | Saturated fat 13g | Total carbs 1g

Net carbs 1g | Protein 124g | Sugars 0g | Fiber 0g | Sodium 1750mg

31. Bacon Cordon Blue

Preparation Time: 30 minutes

Cooking Time: 2 to 2.5 hours

Servings: 6

Ingredients:

- 24 bacon slices
- 3 large boneless, skinless chicken breasts, butterfly
- 3 extra virgin olive oils with roasted garlic flavor
- 3 Yang original dry lab or poultry seasonings
- 12 slice black forest ham; 12-slice provolone cheese

Directions:

1. Using apple or cherry pellets, configure a wood pellet smoker grill for indirect cooking and preheat (180 ° F to 200 ° F) for smoking.

2. Inhale bacon cordon blue for 1 hour.

3. After smoking for 1 hour, raise the pit temperature to 350 ° F.

4. Bacon cordon blue occurs when the internal temperature reaches 165 ° F and the bacon becomes crispy.

5. Rest for 15 minutes under a loose foil tent before serving.

Nutrition:

Calories 956 | Total fat 47g | Saturated fat 13g | Total carbs 1g

Net carbs 1g | Protein 124g | Sugars 0g | Fiber 0g | Sodium 1750mg

32. Roast Duck à I Orange

Preparation Time: 30 minutes

Cooking Time: 2 to 2.5 hours

Servings: 3-4

Ingredients:

- 1 (5-6 lb.) Frozen Long Island, Beijing or Canadian ducks
- 3 tbsp west or 3 tbsp; 1 large orange, cut into wedges
- Three celery stems chopped into large chunks
- Half a small red onion, a quarter; Orange sauce:
- 2 orange cups; 2 tablespoons soy sauce
- 2 tablespoons orange marmalade
- 2 tablespoons honey; 3g tsp grated raw

Directions:

1. Set the wood pellet smoker grill for indirect cooking and use the pellets to preheat to 350 ° F.
2. Roast the ducks at 350 ° F for 2 hours.
3. After 2 hours, brush the duck freely with orange sauce.

4. Roast the orange glass duck for another 30 minutes, making sure that the inside temperature of the thickest part of the leg reaches 165 ° F.

5. Place duck under loose foil tent for 20 minutes before serving.

6. Discard the orange wedge, celery and onion. Serve with a quarter of duck with poultry scissors.

Nutrition:

Calories 956 | Total fat 47g | Saturated fat 13g | Total carbs 1g

Net carbs 1g | Protein 124g | Sugars 0g | Fiber 0g | Sodium 1750mg

33. Herb Roasted Turkey

Preparation Time: 30 minutes (additional 2-3 hours marinade)

Cooking Time: 1 hour 30 minutes

Servings: 2-4

Ingredients:

- 8 Tbsp. Butter, Room Temperature; 3 Tbsp. Butter
- 2 Tbsp. Mixed Herbs Such as Parsley, Sage, Rosemary, And Marjoram, Chopped
- 1/4 Tsp. Black Pepper, Freshly Ground
- 1 (12-14 Lbs.) Turkey, Thawed If pre-frozen

Directions:

1. In a small mixing bowl, combine the 8 tablespoons of softened butter, mixed herbs, and black pepper and beat until fluffy with a wooden spoon.

2. Remove any giblets from the turkey cavity and save them for gravy making, if desired. Wash the turkey, inside and out, under cold running water. Dry with paper towels.

3. Using your fingers or the handle of a wooden spoon, gently push some of the herbed butter underneath the turkey skin onto the breast halves, being careful not to tear the skin.

4. Rub the outside of the turkey with the melted butter and sprinkle with the Traeger Pork and Poultry Rub. Pour the chicken broth in the bottom of the roasting pan.

5. When ready to cook, set temperature to 325 F and preheat, lid closed for 15 minutes.

Nutrition:

Calories 956 | Total fat 47g | Saturated fat 13g | Total carbs 1g

Net carbs 1g | Protein 124g | Sugars 0g | Fiber 0g | Sodium 1750mg

CHAPTER 8:
Appetizer

34. Bacon Cheddar Slider

Preparation Time: 30 minutes

Cooking Time: 15 minutes

Servings: 6-10 (1-2 sliders each as an appetizer)

Recommended pellet: Optional

Ingredients:

- 1-pound ground beef (80% lean)
- 1/2 teaspoon of garlic salt; 1/2 teaspoon salt
- 1/2 teaspoon of garlic; 1/2 teaspoon onion
- 1/2 teaspoon black pepper; 6 bacon slices, cut in half
- ½Cup mayonnaise; Sliced red onion; Ketchup
- 2 teaspoons of creamy wasabi (optional)
- 6 (1 oz) sliced sharp cheddar cheese, cut in half (optional)
- ½Cup sliced kosher dill pickles
- 12 mini breads sliced horizontally

Directions:

1. Place ground beef, garlic salt, seasoned salt, garlic powder, onion powder and black hupe pepper in a medium bowl.

2. Divide the meat mixture into 12 equal parts, shape into small thin round patties (about 2 ounces each) and save.

3. Cook the bacon on medium heat over medium heat for 5-8 minutes until crunchy. Set aside.

4. To make the sauce, mix the mayonnaise and horseradish in a small bowl, if used.

5. Set up a wood pellet smoker grill for direct cooking to use griddle accessories. Contact the manufacturer to see if there is a griddle accessory that works with the wooden pellet smoker grill.

6. Spray a cooking spray on the griddle cooking surface for best non-stick results.

7. Preheat wood pellet smoker grill to 350 ° F using selected pellets. Griddle surface should be approximately 400 ° F.

8. Grill the putty for 3-4 minutes each until the internal temperature reaches 160 ° F.

9. If necessary, place a sharp cheddar cheese slice on each patty while the patty is on the griddle or after the patty is removed from the griddle. Place a small amount of mayonnaise mixture, a slice of red onion, and a hamburger pate in the lower half of each roll. Pickled slices, bacon, and ketchup.

Nutrition:

Calories 77 | Total fat 1g | Saturated fat 1g | Total carbs 17g | Net carbs 15g Protein 3g | Sugars 6g | Fiber 2g | Sodium 14mg | Potassium 243mg

35. Garlic Parmesan Wedge

Preparation Time: 15 minutes

Cooking Time: 30-35 minutes

Servings: 3

Recommended pellet: Optional

- 3 large russet potatoes
- ¼ cup of extra virgin olive oil
- 1 tsp salt
- ¾ teaspoon black hu pepper
- 2 tsp garlic powder
- ¾ cup grated parmesan cheese
- 3 tablespoons of fresh coriander or flat leaf parsley (optional)
- ½ cup blue cheese or ranch dressing per serving, for soaking (optional)

Directions:

1. Gently rub the potatoes with cold water using a vegetable brush to dry the potatoes.
2. Cut the potatoes in half vertically and cut them in half.
3. Wipe off any water released when cutting potatoes with a paper towel. Moisture prevents wedges from becoming crunchy.

4. Put the potato wedge, olive oil, salt, pepper, and garlic powder in a large bowl and shake lightly by hand to distribute the oil and spices evenly.

5. Place the wedges on a single layer of non-stick grill tray / pan / basket (about 15 x 12 inches).

6. Set the wood pellet r grill for indirect cooking and use all types of wood pellets to preheat to 425 degrees Fahrenheit.

7. Put the grill tray in the preheated smoker grill, roast the potato wedge for 15 minutes, and turn. Roast the potato wedge for an additional 15-20 minutes until the potatoes are soft inside and crispy golden on the outside.

8. Sprinkle potato wedge with parmesan cheese and add coriander or parsley as needed. If necessary, add blue cheese or ranch dressing for the dip.

Nutrition:

Calories 87 | Total fat 1g | Saturated fat 2g | Total carbs 27g | Net carbs 15g Protein 3g | Sugars 6g | Fiber 2g | Sodium 14mg | Potassium 143mg

36. Roasted Vegetables

Preparation Time: 20 Minutes

Cooking Time: 20 to 40 Minutes

Servings: 4

Ingredients:

- 1 cup cauliflower floret
- 1 cup small mushroom, half
- One medium zucchini, sliced in half
- One medium yellow squash, sliced in half
- One medium-sized red pepper, chopped to 1.5-2 inches One small red onion, chopped to 1½-2 inch
- ounces small baby carrot
- Six mid-stem asparagus spears, cut into 1-inch pieces
- 1 cup cherry or grape tomato
- ¼ Extra virgin olive oil with cup roasted garlic flavor
- 2 tbsp. of balsamic vinegar
- Three garlic, chopped; 1 tsp. dry time
- 1 tsp. dried oregano
- One teaspoon of garlic salt
- ½ teaspoon black pepper

Directions:

1. Put cauliflower florets, mushrooms, zucchini, yellow pumpkin, red peppers, red onions, carrots, asparagus, and tomatoes in a large bowl.

2. Add olive oil, balsamic vinegar, garlic, thyme, oregano, garlic salt, and black hu to add to the vegetables.

3. Gently throw the vegetables by hand until completely covered with olive oil, herbs, and spices.

4. Spread the seasoned vegetables evenly on a non-stick grill tray/bread/basket (about 15 x 12 inches).

5. Set the wood pellet smoker and grill for indirect cooking and preheat to 425 degrees Fahrenheit using all wood pellets.

6. Transfer the grill tray to a preheated smoker and grill and roast the vegetables for 20-40 minutes or until the vegetables are perfectly cooked. Please put it out immediately.

Nutrition:

Calories: 114 | Carbs: 17g

Fat: 4g | Protein: 3g

37. Grilled Mushroom Skewers

Preparation Time: 5 Minutes

Cooking Time: 60 Minutes

Servings: 6

Ingredients:

- 16 - oz 1 lb. Baby Portobello Mushrooms

For the marinade:

- ¼ - cup olive oil ; ¼ - cup lemon juice
- Small handful of parsley; 1 - tsp sugar
- 1 - tsp salt; ¼ - tsp pepper
- ¼ - tsp cayenne pepper
- 1 to 2 - garlic cloves
- 1 - Tbsp balsamic vinegar

What you will need:

- 10 - inch bamboo/wood skewers

Directions:

1. Add the beans to the plate of a lipped container, in an even layer. Shower the softened spread uniformly out ludicrous, and utilizing a couple of tongs tenderly hurl the beans with the margarine until all around covered.

2. Season the beans uniformly, and generously, with salt and pepper.

3. Preheat the smoker to 275 degrees. Include the beans, and smoke 3-4 hours, hurling them like clockwork or until delicate wilted, and marginally seared in spots.

4. Spot 10 medium sticks into a heating dish and spread with water. It's critical to douse the sticks for in any event 15 minutes (more is better) or they will consume too rapidly on the flame broil.

5. Spot the majority of the marinade fixings in a nourishment processor and heartbeat a few times until marinade is almost smooth.

6. Flush your mushrooms and pat dry. Cut each mushroom down the middle, so each piece has half of the mushroom stem.

7. Spot the mushroom parts into an enormous gallon-size Ziploc sack, or a medium bowl and pour in the marinade. Shake the pack until the majority of the mushrooms are equally covered in marinade. Refrigerate and marinate for 30mins to 45mins.

8. Preheat your barbecue about 300F

9. Stick the mushrooms cozily onto the bamboo/wooden sticks that have been dousing (no compelling reason to dry the sticks). Piercing the mushrooms was a bit of irritating from the outset until I got the hang of things.

10. I've discovered that it's least demanding to stick them by bending them onto the stick. In the event that you simply drive the stick through, it might make the mushroom break.

11. Spot the pierced mushrooms on the hot barbecue for around 3mins for every side, causing sure the mushrooms don't consume to the flame broil. The mushrooms are done when they are delicate; as mushrooms ought to be Remove from the barbecue. Spread with foil to keep them warm until prepared to serve

Nutrition:

Calories: 230 | Carbs: 10g

Fat: 20g | Protein: 5g

CHAPTER 9:
Dessert Recipe

38. S'mores Dip

Preparation Time: 0 Minutes

Cooking Time: 15 Minutes

Servings: 6-8

Ingredients:

- 12 ounces semisweet chocolate chips
- ¼ c. milk
- Two T. melted salted butter
- 16 ounces marshmallows
- Apple wedges
- Graham crackers

Directions:

1. Add wood pellets to your smoker and get your cooker's startup procedure. Preheat your smoker, with your lid closed, until it reaches 450.

2. Put a cast-iron skillet on your grill and add in the milk and melted butter. Stir together for a minute.

3. Cover, and let it smoke for five to seven minutes. The marshmallows should be toasted lightly.

4. Take the skillet off the heat and serve with apple wedges and graham crackers.

Nutrition:

Calories: 90 | Carbs: 15g

Fat: 3g | Protein: 1g

39. Bacon Chocolate Chip Cookies

Preparation Time: 10 Minutes

Cooking Time: 30 Minutes

Servings: 24

Ingredients:

- Eight slices of cooked and crumbled bacon
- 2 ½ t. apple cider vinegar; One t. vanilla
- Two c. semisweet chocolate chips
- Two-room temp eggs; ½ t. baking soda
- One c. granulated sugar; ½ t. salt
- Two ¾ c. all-purpose flour
- One c. light brown sugar
- 1 ½ stick softened butter

Directions:

1. Mix the flour, baking soda, and salt. Cream the sugar and the butter together. Then lower the speed. Add in the eggs, vinegar, and vanilla.

2. Still on low, slowly add in the flour mixture, bacon pieces, and chocolate chips.

3. Add wood pellets to your smoker and follow your cooker's startup method. Preheat your smoker, with your lid closed, until it reaches 375.

4. Place some parchment on a baking sheet and drop a teaspoonful of cookie batter on the baking sheet. Let them cook on the grill,

5. Covered, for approximately 12 minutes or until they are browned.

Nutrition:

Calories: 167 | Carbs: 21g

Fat: 9g | Protein: 2g

40. Cinnamon Sugar Pumpkin Seeds

Preparation Time: 12 Minutes

Cooking Time: 30 Minutes

Servings: 8-12

Ingredients:

- Two T. sugar
- seeds from a pumpkin
- One t. cinnamon
- Two T. melted butter

Directions:

1. Add wood pellets to your smoker and follow your cooker's startup operation. Preheat your smoker, with your lid closed, until it reaches 350.
2. Clean the seeds and toss them in the melted butter. Add them to the sugar and cinnamon. Spread them out on a baking sheet, place on the grill, and smoke for 25 minutes.
3. Serve.

Nutrition:

Calories: 160 | Carbs: 5g

Fat: 12g | Protein: 7g

41. Apple Cobbler

Preparation Time: 20 Minutes

Cooking Time: 1 Hour and 30 Minutes

Servings: 8

Ingredients:

- 8 Granny Smith apples
- One c. sugar
- Two eggs
- Two t. baking powder
- Two c. plain flour
- 1 ½ c. sugar

Directions:

1. Peel and quarter apples, place into a bowl. Add in the cinnamon and one c. sugar. Stir well to coat and let it sit for one hour.

2. Add wood pellets to your smoker and follow your cooker's startup form. Preheat your smoker, with your lid closed, until it reaches 350.

3. Place apples into a Dutch oven. Add the crumble mixture on top and drizzle with melted butter.

4. Place on the grill and cook for 50 minutes.

Nutrition:

Calories: 152 | Carbs: 26g

Fat: 5g | Protein: 1g

42. Pineapple Cake

Preparation Time: 20 Minutes

Cooking Time: 60 Minutes

Servings: 8

Ingredients:

- One c. sugar; One T. baking powder
- One c. buttermilk; Two eggs
- ½ t. salt; ¾ c. brown sugar
- One jar maraschino cherry
- One stick butter, divided
- One can pineapple slice; ½ c. flour

Directions:

1. Add wood pellets to your smoker and observe your cooker's startup procedure. Preheat your smoker, with your lid closed, until it reaches 350.

2. Take a medium-sized cast-iron skillet and melt one half stick butter. Be sure to coat the entire skillet. Sprinkle brown sugar into a cast-iron skillet.

3. Lay the sliced pineapple on top of the brown sugar. Place a cherry into the middle of each pineapple ring.

4. Mix the salt, baking powder, flour, and sugar. Add in the eggs; one-half stick melted butter and buttermilk. Whisk to combine.

5. Put the cake on the grill and cook for an hour.

6. Take off from the grill and let it sit for ten minutes. Flip onto a serving platter.

Nutrition:

Calories: 165 | Carbs: 40g | Fat: 0g | Protein: 1g

CHAPTER 10:
Extra Recipes

43. Ultimate Lamb Burgers

Preparation Time: 20 minutes

Cooking Time: 30 minutes

Servings: 4

Ingredients:

Traeger's: Apple

Burger:

- 2 lbs. ground lamb; 1 jalapeño
- scallions, diced;2 tablespoons mint
- 2 tablespoons dill, minced
- 3 cloves garlic, minced
- Salt and pepper; 4 brioche buns
- 4 slices manchego cheese

Sauce:

- 1 cup mayonnaise
- 2 cloves garlic
- 2 teaspoons lemon juice
- 1 bell pepper, diced;
- salt and pepper

Directions

1. When ready to cook, turn your smoker to 400F and preheat.

2. Add the mint, scallions, salt, garlic, dill, jalapeño, lamb, and pepper to the mixing bowl.

3. Form the lamb mixture into eight patties.

4. Lay the pepper on the grill and cook for 20 minutes.

5. Take the pepper from the grill and place it in a bag, and seal. After ten minutes, remove pepper from the bag, remove seeds and peel the skin.

6. Add the garlic, lemon juice, mayo, roasted red pepper, salt, and pepper and process until smooth. Serve alongside the burger.

7. Lay the lamb burgers on the grill, and cook for five minutes per side, then place in the buns with a slice of cheese, and serve with the homemade sauce.

Nutrition:

- Calories: 50
- Carbs: 4g
- Fiber: 2g
- Fat: 2.5g
- Protein: 2g

44. Citrus- Smoked Trout

Preparation Time: 10 minutes

Cooking Time: 1 to 2 hours

Servings: 6 to 8

Ingredients:

- 6 to 8 skin-on rainbow trout, cleaned and scaled
- 1-gallon orange juice; ¼ cup salt; 1 lemon, sliced
- ½ cup packed light brown sugar
- 1 tablespoon freshly ground black pepper
- Nonstick spray, oil, or butter, for greasing
- 1 tablespoon chopped fresh parsley

Directions:

1. Fillet the fish and pat dry with paper towels
2. Pour the orange juice into a large container with a lid and stir in the brown sugar, salt, and pepper
3. Place the trout in the brine, cover, and refrigerate for 1 hour
4. Cover the grill grate with heavy-duty aluminum foil. Poke holes in the foil and spray with cooking spray

5. Supply your smoker with Traeger's and follow the manufacturer's specific start-up procedure. Preheat, with the lid closed, to 225°F

6. Remove the trout from the brine and pat dry. Arrange the fish on the foil-covered grill grate, close the lid, and smoke for 1 hour 30 minutes to 2 hours, or until flaky

7. Remove the fish from the heat. Serve garnished with the fresh parsley and lemon slices.

Nutrition:

Calories: 220 | Protein: 33 g | Fat: 4 g | Carbohydrates: 17 g

45. Sunday Supper Salmon with Olive Tapenade

Preparation Time: 1 hour and 20 minutes

Cooking Time: 1 to 2 hours

Servings: 10 to 12

Ingredients:

- 2 cups packed light brown sugar
- ½ cup salt; ¼ cup maple syrup
- 1/3 cup crab boil seasoning
- 1 (3- to 5-pound) whole salmon fillet, skin removed
- ¼ cup extra-virgin olive oil; 1 tablespoon dried oregano
- 1 (15-ounce) can pitted green olives, drained
- 1 (15-ounce) can pitted black olives, drained
- 3 tablespoons jarred sun-dried tomatoes, drained
- 3 tablespoons chopped fresh basil
- 2 tablespoons freshly squeezed lemon juice
- 2 tablespoons jarred capers, drained
- 2 tablespoons chopped fresh parsley, plus more for sprinkling

Directions:

1. In a medium bowl, combine the brown sugar, salt, maple syrup, and crab boil seasoning.

2. Rub the paste all over the salmon and place the fish in a shallow dish. Cover and marinate in the refrigerator for at least 8 hours or overnight.

3. Remove the salmon from dish, rinse, and pat dry, and let stand for 1 hour to take off the chill.

4. Meanwhile, in a food processor, pulse the olive oil, green olives, black olives, sun-dried tomatoes, basil, oregano, lemon juice, capers, and parsley to a chunky consistency. Refrigerate the tapenade until ready to serve.

5. Supply your smoker with Traeger's and follow the manufacturer's specific start-up procedure. Preheat, with the lid closed, to 250°F.

6. Place the salmon on the grill grate (or on a cedar plank on the grill grate), close the lid, and smoke for 1 to 2 hours, or until the internal temperature reaches 140°F to 145°F. When the fish flakes easily with a fork, it's done.

7. Remove the salmon from the heat and sprinkle with parsley. Serve with the olive tapenade.

Nutrition:

- Calories: 240;
- Proteins: 23g;
- Carbs: 3g;
- Fat: 16g

46. Grilled Tuna

Preparation Time: 20 minutes

Cooking Time: 4 hours

Servings: 6

Ingredients:

- Albacore tuna fillets – 6, each about 8 ounces
- Salt – 1 cup; Brown sugar – 1 cup
- Orange, zested – 1; Lemon, zested – 1

Directions:

1. Before preheating the grill, brine the tuna, and for this, prepare brine stirring together all of its ingredients until mixed.

2. Take a large container, layer tuna fillets in it, covering each fillet with it, and then let them sit in the refrigerator for 6 hours.

3. Then remove tuna fillets from the brine, rinse well, pat dry and cool in the refrigerator for 30 minutes.

4. When the grill has preheated, place tuna fillets on the grilling rack and let smoke for 3 hours, turning halfway.

5. Check the fire after one hour of smoking and add more wood pallets if required.

6. Then switch temperature of the grill to 225 degrees F and continue grilling for another 1 hour until tuna has turned nicely golden and fork-tender.

7. Serve immediately.

Nutrition:

Calories: 311 | Fiber: 3 g | Saturated Fat: 1.2 g

Protein: 45 g | Carbs: 11 g | Fat: 8.8 g | Sugar: 1.3 g

47. Grilled Swordfish

Preparation Time: 10 minutes

Cooking Time: 18 minutes

Servings: 4

Ingredients:

- Swordfish fillets – 4; Salt – 1 tablespoon
- Ground black pepper – ¾ tablespoon
- Olive oil – 2 tablespoons; Ears of corn – 4
- Cherry tomatoes – 1 pint; Lime, juiced – 1
- Cilantro, chopped – 1/3 cup
- Medium red onion, peeled, diced – 1
- Serrano pepper, minced – 1; Salt – ½ teaspoon
- Ground black pepper – ¼ teaspoon

Directions:

1. In the meantime, prepare fillets and for this, brush them with oil and then season with salt and black pepper.

2. Prepare the corn, and for this, brush with olive oil and season with ¼ teaspoon each of salt and black pepper.

3. When the grill has preheated, place fillets on the grilling rack along with corns and grill corn for 15 minutes until light brown and fillets for 18 minutes until fork tender.

4. When corn has grilled, cut kernels from it, place them into a medium bowl, add remaining ingredients for the salsa and stir until mixed.

5. When fillets have grilled, divide them evenly among plates, top with corn salsa and then serve.

Nutrition: Calories: 311 | Total Fat: 8.8 g | Saturated Fat: 1.2 g

Fiber: 3 g | Protein: 45 g | Sugar: 1.3 g | Carbs: 11 g

48. Lamb Kebabs

Preparation Time: 15 minutes

Cooking Time: 10 minutes

Servings: 4

Ingredients:

Traeger's: Mesquite

- 1/2 tablespoon salt; 2 tablespoons fresh mint
- 3 lbs. leg of lamb; 1/2 cup lemon juice
- 1 tablespoon lemon zest; 15 apricots, pitted
- 1/2 tablespoon cilantro; 2 teaspoons black pepper
- 1/2 cup olive oil;1 teaspoon cumin; 2 red onion

Directions:

1. Combine the olive oil, pepper, lemon juice, mint, salt, lemon zest, cumin, and cilantro. Add lamb leg, then place in the refrigerator overnight.

2. Remove the lamb from the marinade, cube them, and then thread onto the skewer with the apricots and onions.

3. When ready to cook, turn your smoker to 400F and preheat.

4. Lay the skewers on the grill and cook for ten minutes.

5. Remove from the grill and serve.

Nutrition:

- Calories: 50
- Carbs: 4g
- Fiber: 2g
- Fat: 2.5g
- Protein: 2g

49. Special Occasion's Dinner Cornish Hen

Preparation Time: 15 Minutes

Cooking Time: 1 Hour

Servings: 4

Ingredients:

- 4 Cornish game hens
- Four fresh rosemary sprigs
- 4 tbsp. butter, melted
- 4 tsp. chicken rub

Directions:

1. Set the temperature of Traeger Grill to 375 degrees F and preheat with a closed lid for 15 mins.
2. With paper towels, pat dries the hens.
3. Tuck the wings behind the backs, and with kitchen strings, tie the legs together.
4. Coat the outside of each hen with melted butter and sprinkle with rub evenly.
5. Stuff the cavity of each hen with a rosemary sprig.
6. Place the hens onto the grill and cook for about 50-60 mins.
7. Remove the hens from the grill and place onto a platter for about 10 mins.

8. Cut each hen into desired-sized pieces and serve.

Nutrition:

Calories per serving: 430 | Carbohydrates: 2.1g

Protein: 25.4g | Fat: 33g | Sodium: 331mg | Fiber: 0.7g

50. Crispy and Juicy Chicken

Preparation Time: 15 Minutes

Cooking Time: 5 Hours

Servings: 6

Ingredients:

- ¾ C. dark brown sugar
- ½ C. ground espresso beans
- 1 tbsp. ground cumin
- 1 tbsp. ground cinnamon
- 1 tbsp. garlic powder
- 1 tbsp. cayenne pepper
- Salt and freshly ground black pepper
- 1 (4-lb.) whole chicken, neck and giblets removed

Directions:

1. Set the temperature of Traeger Grill to 200-225 degrees F and preheat with a closed lid for 15 mins.
2. In a bowl, mix brown sugar, ground espresso, spices, salt, and black pepper.
3. Rub the chicken with spice mixture generously.
4. Put the chicken onto the grill and cook for about 3-5 hours.

5. Remove chicken from grill and place onto a cutting board for about 10 mins before carving.

6. With a sharp knife, cut the chicken into desired sized pieces and serve.

Nutrition:

Calories per serving: 540 | Carbohydrates: 20.7g | Protein: 88.3g

Fat: 9.6g | Sugar: 18.1g | Sodium: 226mg | Fiber: 1.2g

9 781803 011509